Suddenly It's Evening

Selected Poems

T0079895

Books by John Skoyles

Poetry
A Little Faith
Permanent Change
Definition of the Soul
The Situation

Prose
Generous Strangers
Secret Frequencies: A New York Education
A Moveable Famine: A Life in Poetry

Suddenly It's Evening

Selected Poems

John Skoyles

Carnegie Mellon University Press
Pittsburgh 2016

Acknowledgments

The author and publisher wish to thank editors of the following journals and anthologies in which poems in this selection were first published:

Agni Review, American Poetry Review, The Antioch Review, Ark River Review, The Atlantic Monthly, Boulevard, Chicago Review, Gaia, Georgia Review, Harvard Review, Iowa Review, Ironwood, Italian Americana, Many Mountains Moving, The Missouri Review, New Myths/MSS, North American Review, Ohio Review, Orion, Outsiders, Ploughshares, Poetry, Poetry East, River City, Shankpainter, Slate, Sonora Review, TriQuarterly, Virginia Quarterly Review, Warren Wilson Review, Washington Square, Whispering Campaign, The Yale Review

The Ardis Anthology of New American Poetry (Ardis), *The Poetry Anthology 1902–2002: Ninety Years of America's Most Distinguished Verse Magazine* (Ivan R. Dee), *New American Poets of the 80s* (Wampeter Press), *The Carnegie-Mellon Anthology of Poetry* (Carnegie-Mellon University Press), *Cape Discovery: Twenty-five years of Writing from the Fine Arts Work Center* (Sheep Meadow Press), *Articulations: The Body and Illness in Poetry* (The University of Iowa Press), *Stepping Out: Poems about Hotels, Motels, Restaurants and Bars* (Milkweed Editions), *Ethical Decision Making in Nursing* (W.B. Saunders Company), *Hammer & Blaze: A Gathering of Contemporary American Poets* (University of Georgia Press), *Perfect in Their Art: Poems on Boxing from Homer to Ali* (Southern Illinois University Press), *Broken Land: Poems of Brooklyn* (New York University Press), *Enskyment Anthology* (Cook Communication), *Aspects of Robinson: Homage to Weldon Kees* (The Backwaters Press), *New Hungers from Old: One-Hundred Years of Italian-American Poetry* (Star Cloud Press)

Cover art: Paul Resika; *Calabash Moonlight, II*; 2008; oil on canvas; 40 x 48 inches

Book cover image courtesy of the artist and Lori Bookstein Fine Art, New York.

Book design: Connie Amoroso

for Jerry Costanzo

Contents

from *Definition of the Soul*

from *The Situation*

Each of us is alone on the heart of the earth
pierced by a ray of sunlight:
and suddenly it's evening.

—Salvatore Quasimodo

from *A Little Faith*

The Business of Dying

I don't care at all who died today.
There's not a single reason
to list the deaths today.
Maybe my father opens the sports page,
or my mother a mystery novel
in New York this afternoon,
a place where on another day
I could follow death like a woman
into the subway, where death
is just a headline, where boys
light freezing derelicts on fire.

So let's forget who died today,
the families, their keepsakes,
the clumsy last breaths.
Because this afternoon I know
I've invested my heart in good places,
that if this woman drops off to sleep
right now I'll still be here exhaling,
feeling guilty but lucky,
like a man with no connections.

Because someone left for work today
loving his children, but cursing his life,
and some union men, on strike again,
lounged in a tavern,
lost count of their beers
as I've lost track of these hours,
this afternoon, the days I've run through,
and the woman who moved me
this far, so far from my death.

In Memoriam

We stayed in a resort town that Easter
and walked the beach at low tide,
eyeing what was left behind.
I was with a woman
whose mother had just died.
She seemed less a daughter than a souvenir,
a keepsake bringing back
a familiar, "Remember that?"

The motel recalled my room as a boy
where a dog slept beneath the bed.
Driftwood twisted on the wall.
We put out cigarettes
in an ashtray of shell.

She kept thinking about the past
while I couldn't help
imagining her years later,
the way you run into childhood friends
and the rings of their parents
appear on their hands.

At night I read late,
listening to the waves outside.
The rising and falling was punctual,
obsessed, like the routine
of someone about to break down.
She slept a lot, said little,
and imitated, I thought,
some gestures of her mother.

I never felt like a man there,
and, before turning out the light,
I placed a glass of water
beside the bed,
as if it had been brought
in the middle of the night

If You Have an Enemy

If you have an enemy, picture him asleep.
Notice his shoes by the side of the bed,

how helplessly they gape there.
Some mornings he needs three cups of coffee

to wake up for work,
and there are evenings he drinks alone,

reading the paper down to the want ads,
the arrival times of ships at the docks.

Think of him choosing a tie,
dialing wrong numbers,

finding holes in his socks.
Chances are his emptiness

equals yours when you thoughtlessly
hurry a cashier for change,

or frown to yourself in rush hour traffic,
and the drivers behind you

begin to remind you
the light has turned green.

Guilt

I know it's dark inside us.
I'm sure we all feel haunted
by an absence of light.
Don't think I'm a believer
in original sin, but that woman
putting her plants in the sun
imagines the deep carpets in hotel suites,
and the boy sorting dirty postcards
in the night is so close to his needs
his body is an echo of the dark inside it.

I guess we all have a skeleton
in the closet, a secret
that drives us from the warmth of home.
Because under dim streetlights
the brokenhearted wander
from corner to corner,
and in theatres the abandoned
settle softly in the dark
like kittens at the bottom of a pool.

And although the priests are urging us
to confess everything we've done,
I think we're grateful
for what we don't know about each other:
the past that's with us like a grudge,
the guilt we're feeling and god knows why.

Dear John

It's wonderful to see you here again.
I heard you were half-dead
from loving someone back in Chicago,
but the part that's living seems twice as alive.
Yet you're a little pale
from standing in front of the mirror too long—
you have that sullen look I've seen
on men in love with the same woman.

Please remember that I've missed you.
You haven't been yourself lately,
you've forgotten who you are:
you're no star, but you're popular.
As a boy you always did what you were told
and all the teachers kissed you.

I was proud of you then,
for keeping those magazines in the cellar
and passing them around.
So when the nuns made you head
of the Boy Savior Club,
all the kids said,
"Everyone thinks John's an angel."

And when you led the class in prayer,
keeping a straight face
even to your closest friend,
I loved you then.
But it's funny seeing you now
in a room full of strangers,
and you'll be the last to leave,
if I know you.

We've come so far to be near
each other today,

I'd like to say I love you,
but forgive me, I'm too shy,
and can only love you now
through someone else's eyes.

Burlesque

after Weldon Kees

The day the dancer in the loud red dress
tossed her hair and asked, "What else is there to do?"
I remembered what my father told me.
She looked into the mirror applying makeup
while the traffic lights went on and off outside.

What my father told me was this:
women look into mirrors looking for men;
blondes toss their hair indifferently all night
but finally settle down; changes of heart
flicker like the traffic lights.

We fall in and out of love in rooms
where women wearing makeup
reflect our fantasies and lust,
so we're to blame for whatever they become.
And looking back, how could we

have taken that dancer so seriously?
But the way to forget
how she stepped out of her dress
was something our fathers couldn't tell us.
The lights go on and go off.

Invective Against Blondes

The body, my darlings, yearns beyond kisses
and far beyond the distraction of a bed.

A white shower of wedding rice might end
the years of looking, the time you tried out

ballplayers, playwrights, the average guy—
men who slept better when you were gone,

and were not surprised to have heard you say,
"While you were away, I fell for Fred."

Be careful, already at their endless chores,
the wives of friends seem more or less alike.

And the body, my darlings, sleeps half its life
like a cat in an armchair, like an unhappy wife.

Snowstorm in the Country

Things are bad: birds outside my window eat snow.
I'm surrounded by trees, and children in the orchard
bully each other by climbing high,
higher than the smaller boys
who pick at the rough bark and wander off.

And there's a girl in braids who needs a boost
to the lowest branch.
She stays below, covered in snow,
a cold and lovely figure in this world of boys,
their inspiration, or their terror of it, I don't know.

Knockout

Sometimes two people together
cancel each other out,
and are left dizzy and alone,
as if hesitating near an office door
where they might not be wanted.
Those seconds so conspicuous,
slower than the whole long day,
just like that instant in a slow round
when a good left connects,
and the crowd so silent
before it sinks in
that even the aggressor takes a while
to follow it up. And who knows,
his opponent might want to be alone now,
now that the boredom of vertical life
has tasted him, pulling him down
the way God floored St. Teresa
so she woke up not recognizing anyone,
but content she went through
something glorious and came out even.

No Thank You

Who'll be the lover of that woman on the bench?
If she wants to hurt someone, she can use me.

Did she mean it, or was she trying to be unforgettable?
If she wants to use someone, she can hurt me.

I'll use my manners to stay in one piece,
but I end up believing every excuse that I make.

I always sigh when I see a woman like this.
I don't know where it comes from, and I don't know where it goes.

I thought I'd enjoy a beautiful day like today.
I took a walk in the park and then something like this happens.

I Don't Want to Hear Anymore about Love

I'd rather watch the junkman
arrange his new piece of junk,
or remember the way I felt as a child
holding my mother's hand in traffic.
There's a certain trust in these things
that I like, a mindless greed,
an unanswered lust, the kind
everyone knows is dead
but some poor soul keeps trying to revive.

So I don't want to hear anymore about love,
unless it's a particularly one-sided love,
possessive love, love immobilized
by need, love with no chance
of fulfillment, a love so helpless
and frail it can only be kissed
and put to bed,
a love that needs someone
to wake it.

Queens, New York

In the neighborhood where I was born,
my friends have stationed tiny saints
on the dashboards of their cars,
relics from St. Joan of Arc's
where nuns were married to a god
who seemed cruel, but possibly true,
like rumors about Sharon O'Rourke
who crossed her legs and blew smoke rings
toward the classroom ceiling after school.

We dreamt of becoming presidents
while our fathers fell asleep in chairs
after three beers, an eight-hour day
and nine innings of the Yankees on TV.
Each Saturday they'd visit barbershops,
trade tips on horses or the stock exchange,
and relive disasters like the crash of '29,
when bankrupt brokers jumped off roofs
and sank in the tar like dimes on a hot day.

Rush hour took everyone underground
and on weekends we joined crowds
of families driving toward the shore,
sometimes stalled by limousines
surrounding a chapel that seemed out of place
for hosting a funeral on a sunny day.
The mourning relatives, dutiful and black,
darkened the sidewalk with lengths of shade,
as if the shadows of the dead were still alive,

like feelings we bury but still kiss goodbye.

Kilcullen & Murray's

for Keith Althaus

I take the stool
between the fat lady
bellowing Sophie Tucker
and the Irishman's Al Jolson,
near the obliterating jazz
and the merciful bartender,
because with the clinics,
rest homes and funeral parlors,
with the news
and the news behind the news,
with these people who are disappointed
every New Year's Eve,
and who are always facing spring alone,
you get tired of being serious.

Saturday Night & Sunday Morning

in memory of Michael Sheridan

You've fallen asleep with a drink
in your hand, goodnight.
Dream about me, your other friends,
and remember we catch cold,
call someone ours, and look out
the window alone. Then wake your wife
when sunlight breaks, and chase
your daughters from the guest room door.
Let me sleep late.

Through the hangovers and growing pains,
I can't forget your youngest daughter,
upset at last night's late show
despite the thrill of the hour,
adult laughter, and a new face
telling jokes. She took the movie
so seriously, she said today on the phone
to her friend, *There were funny parts,*
but it was sad at the end.

Hard Work

This morning I have awakened in New York
while the population of California still sleeps.
A woman I once knew very well
pulls the covers around her shoulders
in Los Angeles, while I buy the paper
and a coffee-to-go
in this city where we lived together.

This room was ours, we shared it,
and used to lie in bed and guess
who cried behind these plaster walls,
who stumbled on the stairs late at night.

This morning as I woke up in New York,
schoolboys at bus stops discussed
the facts of life, and the headlines said
there's a plane crash in the south,
those passengers seated beside each other
gone to different cemeteries
without exchanging another word.

This room was ours, but I kept all of it,
daydream near the electric fan,
visit those tenants who kept us awake
and play cards with them,
sullen men with nothing on their minds
but the good luck that deals them
three of a kind, the bad luck
that makes them experts at bluffing.

In the Depot

I thought I saw you in the depot
though you were living in another city.

I don't like to make mistakes like that,
and I didn't care for the panhandler

who mistook my confusion
for a bewildered out-of-towner's

and recited hard luck stories
for some change. Worse, he asked

about that look in my eye,
guessed something was wrong,

a beggar's ancient line,
but I was so stunned

by your sudden appearance
I forgot the brusque phrases

for keeping my distance
I'd practiced so carefully.

from *Permanent Change*

Good Cheer

My mother called all street vendors
by one name: the little men,
and preferred stopping there
to Woolworth's or Schrafft's.
"How about some chestnuts from the little man?"
she'd say, after a gruesome round
through holiday crowds at Macy's.
That phrase first struck me odd
ten years after I heard it:
my father in the hospital,
I came home from college
to comfort my mother.
After one visit, when we left
in early evening, and limousines
and sports cars from New Jersey
headed toward the East Side bars,
she said, "Should we go home, or stop
for something from the little man?"
I loved her for bringing back
that old routine, freshly heard,
just as we verged on permanent change.
I worried so much about my father's heart,
my mother's false good cheer,
that every commonplace seemed significant,
and every significance, absurd.
We stood under a loud umbrella
signed *Sabrett's* in a whirling script
and I ordered.
It was the first time, too, I really looked
at my mother: all smiles
in a full-length fake fur coat
with a real fur collar.
And myself: the jacket and tie
chosen for a style

imitating the Ivy League.
The little man, pleased to serve us,
made a serious production
above the mustard well,
and with a serious flourish
snapped the tissue from the straw.
Then we returned to our apartment
in Queens, to a street
where women always seemed to be sweeping,
and no one shook
when glass and metal crashed,
as if they expected it.

White Nights

after Montale

There are those who live
in a time that's touched them.
They stay shocked

by a death or a kiss
and won't walk away,
won't speak from the heart

or stand too long near anyone.
Love took them by surprise
although they circled first

like beasts before a fight.
The world saw two people
going though one door.

Soon one wouldn't open
that door to the other.
Yet the icy smirker can't sleep

and there's a hush
inside the one who still loves
as inside a room

when someone's expected.
Strange what makes them shudder,
afraid to cry, pick up the phone

or just walk outside.
One evening an old photo
from an album

stuns unnaturally hard
and there is no darkness
when they close their eyes.

Elegy in Autumn

A bad dream left me with the words
"Remove a dead leaf with a dead leaf,"
and I recalled that line in the brittle fall
as I crossed the cemetery's maze
in the throes of disentangling
your unpopular grave
from the rest of the bleary tombs.
Each path beneath the crackling
airy leaves was painful,
as if they were lives or loves I walked on.
With surgical care,
I sidestepped the inhabited shapes,
through air like the scent
of my parents' bed
where I crawled as a child.
A thick white bicycle, scuffed and half-twisted,
leaned on the mailbox of the gatekeeper's trailer,
appealing to me the way
my childhood's sleek racer did not—was that the leaf,
to prefer the used thing, the abandoned one?
I turned from the must and cobble of the graveyard
into downtown's flamboyant light
where I hoped to retrieve your face
from the confiscating earth.
Music shouted for a second from a door
where a couple entered,
for a split second when someone brisked in alone.
It was the day after you were buried
and wind blasted the street leaves high
in the seasonal gap
between looking forward and looking back.

My Dead

Out of the sparks from the fireplace
appear the shuffling dead.
One cinder that shoots by
and scrapes around before flaring out
has me turning my head,
thinking my grandmother entered the room
in her thick shoes,
carrying a plate of toast.
Back on Judge Street,
she sat in an armchair
cutting beanbags and rugged dolls
out of thick upholstery.
Her roofer husband died in a fall
from the tarred slant of the Jack Frost building,
leaving eight kids and a cottage industry
that reached its height
when she restitched a hat
for Guy Lombardo's wife.
That last year I'd call and listen hard
to the ring of her phone,
knowing the number would be
disconnected soon, and after her death
I dialed again, superstitiously,
though AT&T efficiently assigned
that number to Sid's: A House of Clothes.
Although it goes against my training,
I don't pray for her, or ask her
to intercede for me
to lift the heat and friction
from which she's freed.

Dark Card

Grief that lingers begins to mock,
and I started to feel extravagant scorn
for the sluggish chat brought on
by flowers splayed like open hands,
her fundamental rouge, and the cold
that trailed everyone's coat
through the putty-like air
of the small funeral home.
I missed the quick encapsulating glee
with which she spoke,
rushing everything together
in the energetic tongue
of those who live alone.
There had been two of her:
one whose office overlooked bronze Atlas
hauling the world on his back,
where she twisted dull and courteous speech
into perfect frenzy on a steno pad.
The other cleared the dinner table
then cut the tarot deck,
warning it was an ancient fraud
but frowning when she turned a dark card.
I see her pointing again
to the picture of a tea service in disarray
and saying, "There will be talk."
A long grief buckles and breaks
into fantasy, and the loved one
tugs you closer and closer.

Times Square

"She looks just like a doll lying there,"
my Aunt Linda said when I walked
into her office at Paramount Pictures.
She had been staring out the window
at the body of a prostitute
crumpled five floors below
on the marquee of the Strand Hotel,
where an ecstatic clientele bickered
at the windows like wasps against glass.
Somewhere else forsythia bloomed
that April but, for me, it was working
as a messenger on Times Square,
where almost everyone in the mailroom
caught the clap on lunch hour.
I bought a fake star sapphire ring
for five dollars, and watched the star fade,
then the stone itself peel away
until I could see a kind of face
mimicking my most puzzled expression
in its sickly oval sky.

Holy Cross Church

West 42nd Street

Nothing in here has the simple
cut-rate clarity of the street,
where storefronts display
school rings and saxophones,
and theatres jab their lewd marquees
into an avenue of bargaining.
I used to rest here,
joining a few men and women
who clasped and unclasped their hands
in a pew, thanking and asking.

A sign announced the Sunday sermon.
I remember "The Foolishness of God"
and feeling odd about sweating
under the closed eyes of agonized saints.
Noisy men by the holy water font
impressed each other
with the names of distant cities,
dividing their stories
into two insistent types:
the truth, and the God's honest truth.

I fell somewhere between those lies,
and often lit a candle
for a relative or friend.
The rootless flame swayed back and forth,
bearing its namesake along a draft
caught between worlds,
overpowered and led here
by which wrong direction,
hopefulness or despair?

Corona Avenue

A pack of otherworldly, scuffling souls
picked through the streets,
as if spun from a whirlwind of vapors.

Near the trestle, three thugs
harmonized in a doorway
while an entire engine

hung from a limb.
If you found yourself staring
at Teresa Cole a little too long,

then you were in trouble
with Big Jim Flem.
If you found yourself rolling in the weeds

with Noreen Ketchum,
you were in luck too good to be true—
she flaunted a beehive perm,

a chipped tooth, and a tattoo.
With a razor,
I carved her nickname, Raven,

into my upper arm,
a sign of love so mangled
no one could read it,

and lucky for me,
I was already the laughingstock
of Corona Avenue.

Self-Portrait in Spring

I wade into the water and look around:
nothing, just the same pair of eyes
staring inward, the same voice
describing myself. Suddenly
there's a commotion far out,
a noisy capture or escape.
The ocean shivers for a second
like a restless subconscious
while I stand very still,
a wave that can't break. Everywhere
a blue-black ache for the shore,
and on the ocean floor,
half-exposed by a strong undertow,
something buried works hard at getting home.

On the Train

Nobody looks familiar today; it has snowed.
The commuters are slightly incognito,
spies from past holidays,
wearing useful gifts against the cold.
How cruel and anonymous the sky seems,
like a caller claiming credit for a bombing.
I'm sure I recognize a visiting aunt,
and my old alcoholic boss,
but when they get closer, no, they change.
Snow has turned a white dog gray.

Restless landscape, blurry, impenetrable,
from the ponds and aviaries
of the very rich, to hillsides
where they stack the wrecks in pairs,
make by make, year upon year. . . .

The smoking car fills with the beautiful smell
of lighter fluid,
and the entering passengers look public and bored
like the faces on change.
I've acquired the vices of the passerby:
the private slouch around a paper cup,
appraisal and envy of what stays in one place.

In this way we leave city after city,
name upon name,
and those of us who have said good-bye
with an unusual vehemence
find the figures standing at each station
resemble each other,
straight from the heat
inside that claustrophobic pronoun we,
plural and alone.

Snowfall

This could be any city, the poor part,
poverty both camouflaged and signaled
by unplowed snow. The morning paper
still lies on the doorstep,
touched only by the cold gloves
of a boy who moves in his own world
from house to house, past a shadow
pulling a sweater on, to a woman
who answers her door in a slip.
Never have our neighbors been so stranded
in their past. One tries to get to work
and the sound of his footfalls
is surprisingly loud,
like pages turned in waiting rooms.
Another stands by a window
as the falling snow continues to erase
these streets where no one important lives,
leaving just the crooked shapes
of cars and houses, white silhouettes,
a background drifting forward, nothing else.

The Repairman

When he begins his small talk,
surprising passions are revealed—
hatred of the mandolin,
steam heat and housecats.
I am standing in a yard
packed with washers and dryers
and have just bought one of each.
Where others have been trucked off,
dead patches grid the lawn
so it seems we are surrounded
by survivors in a board game.
He adds up the cost
of a nearly new agitator,
a very big spring,
parts saved
to make something from nothing.
I can't help compare myself
to this man, Mr. Moore:
his prizing of age
to a precious degree,
the frank manhandling
with which he divides
the redeemable from the junk.
He shows me a barn
where he files the rust
off gizmos I can't name
while I ramble on,
linking one farfetched
coincidence to the next.
Neither of us has been kissed
by lady luck,
so we face each other
on this weedy showroom floor,
and when a neighbor's car
starts its high sick whistling,

that sound echoes through both of us,
and through the barren
hallucinatory roads
that led us here.

Front Street

Neither of us had an easy winter
though it must have looked like it,
sitting at a window on the bay
with glasses of whiskey.
The low tide brought birdlife, dogs,
bits of clay or porcelain plate,
and tourists taking the lazy way to town.
High tide covered everything
right up to the porch, and one day
we lost our tempers over it.
Arguing with the powers of the moon
is a losing business, and by spring
he went off to a high-paying job,
AA meetings and no time
even to breathe the sea air.
I left to teach in a floral suburb
with the same detriments.
The tides don't miss us,
nor the landlord who owned
that waterfront property,
nor Gerald the cat
who we squirted with pistols
when he crept up on the tern nests.
And Susan and Shelley, where are they?
The sea and its tides
must be having a laugh
on the two guys who fell
for their heroic example,
fatal to mortals,
of starting over and over again.

The Head of Tasso

Three sisters lived downstairs,
Anne, Florence and Sarah,
all in their eighties,
each of them ill for weeks at a time.
When Florence died,
I wrote a note of sympathy,
a recollection of the worried grace
with which she stalked
our building's strangers through the stairwells
and tailed the elusive landlord
with a thesis of complaint.
In her will I received
a woodcut of the head of Tasso,
a fiery print her sisters said
any museum would be happy to have.
I learned Tasso took a blow
to the head and after whirled
the streets in insane fits,
but I hung the portrait.
Its afflicted face,
like a horse's suddenly
pulled to a halt,
looked out the window
at a fire escape burglars used,
the news of which
shook the remaining sisters
who disappeared almost overnight
as if ascending
through a single sleeve of sunlight.
Fastidious, kind, with a roving paranoia
that plowed blood through their veins,
they used to stand in their foyer
of fake roses, tearing petals
to place beneath the bouquets
so they appeared to have dropped there,
once alive.

Symmetry

Number three, childhood's unlucky figure,
intentionally ditched
around a corner,
rose up to brand Dean Bender,
chronic third party of the seventh grade.
A sweet-tempered stutterer slow to answer,
he scratched his nose as he stood by his desk
for such long seconds
it seemed we were on a train
and everyone looked outside.
When he fought a squat thug after class,
everyone booed him, larger of the two.
With each punch he threw,
the crowd chanted, "Duh-duh-duh-Dean!"
Every day a hurt boy walked out of the schoolyard,
and on every wall spray paint
raged the fame of local lovers.
For years Dean ushered at the matinee,
cultivated his love of ham radio
and King Tut, never noticing
everyone moved away in pairs
that spun off a third.
His father on the vice squad
totaled up how many he booked each night,
how many cigarettes smoked.
Mr. Bender had two kids for the sake of symmetry:
Dean and a girl
who used to pound her head against the wall.

Men Versus Men

December 20, 1963

This was before much talk of a third world,
and the working classes wore away
shovelful by shovelful
as the city grew taller.
I was in bed with my father,
pillows propped up,
watching the Friday night fights
and Gillette's cartoon parrot
flash the rounds
on a giant safety razor.
Twenty-two years later,
a small piece in the *Times*
recalls the knockout:
2 minutes and 13 seconds,
a precise mathematical notation
hidden in the slop and sweat
of a forgotten life.
For the two faces staring
diagonally across a canvas mat,
it was business as usual:
both black, one maligned
for killing an opponent in the ring.
The other later serving time.
I like knowing where I was that night.
It made me live over again
an age when I thought of nothing
but men versus men.
Back there, my father and I
praised the jazzed-up anthem
aimed at the rafters,
and afterward,
the deft, almost archeological
effort to coax a man back
from his twitching oblivion.

Against Autumn

Survivors return to the place
where something terrible happened,
crippled and set free
by the deaths around them.
They know they'll go too someday
so they won't go quietly,
and in this knowledge they stand out
like trees you never notice until autumn,
when the plain ones rage
and the common maple
seems to set our hats and coats on fire.
It's a season bothered by untimely deaths
and looking too carefully
for coincidence and signs.
A trail of party hats blows across
the expressway, and the traffic
seems suddenly exuberant, giddy.
Everyone marks death with bright fruit
from dry fields, fruit with a sweetness
too much like decay, and speckled gourds,
the spidery freaks of some rural imagination.
Autumn, when whole stadiums smolder,
and children, when you kiss them,
taste like the wind.
We have survived the pleadings
of the summer street
with its sirens, hysteria and beer.
Leaves hang in twos and threes
like long-saved ornaments
at the corners of a tree.
Under that burly, disheveling sky,
mothers tell children life starts from a seed.

Night After Night

In early spring when we first met,
and our fingers still had that wintry touch
of things buried under the snow,
her daughter brought
two tadpoles home from school.
They looked as if it hurt to grow,
the way they held their wobbly heads
sideways, and mouthed bubbles
that seemed to stand for words.
As I refilled our drinks and cracked
fresh ice night after night,
they grew unblinkingly resigned
to the cold flashes of refrigerated light.
The air around that jar of fronds,
sand and half-formed things
gave off a scent so much like death
you could mistake it for life.

3 a. m.

What I mistook for whispering in the yard
were two oil drums split by a breeze,
a looping wind that bewildered
the trees, rocked a nest so it fell,
an overthrown crown of mud and vine.
A sparrow returned and scraped its beak
twice on the forked limb.
It didn't hazard around
but remained dignified and still
locking us both under a dead-center moon
and harangued by those zealots
of late-night fiascos, the mockingbirds,
imitating a houseful of hinges.
How many eggs spilled under the nest,
how many threads of hers and mine
woven into the toppled ounces?
I entered the hours
that bring years, and with the years,
what the years bring.

from *Definition of the Soul*

Definition of the Soul

The attempt to separate my soul from yours
is like wringing out a handkerchief
wet from something spilled.

I remember the burned-down house
where a wreath still hung on the door,
a wreath, stone-white to our surprise,
useless, forlorn, like a life preserver
nailed to the shore's churning rubble.

You said the flames went off somewhere,
strengthened, more vile than ever,
perhaps seeking a child's crib.

When speeding tires lofted street water
onto your dress, I admired how you. . . .

And afterward, I brushed your hair,
as you lay dozing on the couch,
your lower lip, a perfect, promising V.

The attempt to separate my soul from yours
is like the creaking of a lamppost
against a sapling in the wind.
Soon someone will come
and hack through the more fragile one.

Marina

Her name alone,
so strange and lean,
I loved to repeat,
and the time she dove
from the flying bridge
into the white-tipped waves
shook me all the more
for the leaves of salad
and whole buns floating
among the dreck
under the Throgs Neck Bridge.
We finished that day
at Louie's German Beer Stadium
where baseball blared
and little boys
peeked through the shabbier
end of the bathhouse.
When she gestured with her wrist,
her silver bangles
rang with the sound
of coins falling to the floor,
which I kept stooping to retrieve.
And just as foolishly,
I snapped my head
to the open air,
feeling something
had flown by,
a hornet or a wren,
and when I stood there alone,
I felt again its full strength
and speed.

New Year

The new calendar's brazen grid
begs for notations to deface
its field, not the jottings of time
and place but the scrawl
etched by blades across a pond
of ice, script-like, so you want
to crack the code.
It says: in a new year
confetti has a chance
to reincarnate as a page;
that the foam's big dream
to join the body of the beer
might come true;
that splinters pinched
from a toddler's palm
might resurrect into a spear
of kindling for a flame
where we could warm ourselves
until the rambunctious months
of spring arrive, the buds,
the bursting tufts that touch
the air without excuse,
unlike my glove that holds you up
along the crippling ice
and cushions any feeling for the bone.

Beacon Hill

I can still feel
the twist of her hips
down the stairs,
her hair shielding
whatever her heart
has done to her face.

And the room
where we placed each other
over a narrow bed,
the sheets creased
like a palm
stretched toward a gypsy—

see the lines there,
the braided paths
that trailed off
into weddings and bursts
of fresh power—
and once,

the sight of her
on a bicycle
ticking down a row
of shops,
then pausing at a display
of lush stationery,

watermarked,
and pressed
by an array
of quartz paperweights
fractured in half
to expose their beauty.

After Surgery

Walking the hall
was like circling the dance floor
the night Piggy's got strobe lights.
Just as you sidestepped the waitress
she clanged you with her tray,
the eclipse too quick
for those of us laboring
under the ruling constellations,
slaving like ice in tumblers of gin.
A codeine sleep our sole release
except for baseball,
a pleasure wrecked all week
by the ubiquitous presence
of a part-time catcher from Chicago
named Karkovice
whose name boiled up in fever dreams
as a refrain
that tugged my head
from one side of the bed to the other.
Karkovice, a voodoo doctor
mixing a potion called "Jazz Drool."
Karkovice, the tarpit that flummoxed
the last mastodon.
Karkovice, the phrase, in Stupka,
for "more than enough."
Karkovice, the thick lip
that drops off a highway
when the dirt road begins.

Mop String

Everything in my hospital room
remained photograph still
during my two-week stay
except for the stray inch of string
pushed loose from the mop
by the maid's exuberant sloshing.
Pet-like, it hid in a new corner
each day, dragged to the door
by the surgeon's half-pound brogan,
or plastered to the molding,
a convict pinned against
the perimeter wall
to evade the searchlight—
parched, doused, stiffened again
with a pine scent.
I picked it up just before
they wheeled me out.
Sunlight leapt upon the windows
of the airport bus,
onto rows of bandaged passengers
pressing their incisions
at each sharp turn,
and the pungent inch,
the rough charm
that kept me company
while my drilled skull throbbed,
seemed lost, not saved,
as it unfurled along the lifeline
of my palm.

Unlucky Corner

Unlucky corner where sleet drools
down the silver sides of busses

and snowplows hammer knee-deep slush
at the door of the pet store

that replaced the deli
which stood where the fern bar died.

Corner of no streetlight,
where kids blink at the overbearing sky,

and crushing treads round
a gorged veer that bends

into the railroad yard,
a curve like the racetrack's final turn,

the place where wallets cry.
Corner where I first thought

of leaving here for good,
never again looking both ways

over and over
as the stream from the stifled drains

sneaked up, corner where my small
son's grin spanned the clouds,

all cheeks and teeth bucking out his mouth.
Unlucky corner of cascading sleaze

pushing the boulevard's refuse
to the pike,

corner where a nun sits all summer
in the shade of her enormous hat

shaped like a flying buttress,
with a bowl in her lap.

Winter corner where ice conspires
with the curb against flesh and bone,

where any season,
whether you are happy or unhappy,

it is impossible to cross alone.

Midlife

Halfway through life, one begins looking back.

And you see a hodge podge
of gravediggers, bookies and stenographers,
uncles leaning over linguini
at a dive called Vagabondo,
terriers, a garden with a patio,
the nylon and hollow lawn chairs
of two maiden aunts,
telephones bringing news of death,
the stoop where you split your lip,
the street where you roller-skated
on the arm of a priest,
now strewn with crack vials
and the bodies of the chafed,
the long dead fig tree
your grandmother posed against,
holding her summer cache of five fruits,
the mafia in-law hit by a cab
near a casino, and your own life
growing and fraying,
like a ball made of rubber bands
you found just yesterday
in the back of a drawer, and recalled
how it lost and gained momentum
with the shape of the road
you walked with your friends
who one by one
made their ways and their names
which soon stood above them on a stone.

Elegy for Munro Moore

1927-1995

My friend Munro sailed alone
from Provincetown,
a pastel gloom
hailed in a slogan
as "the last resort."
His boat was the *Blue Moon*.
His compass pointed north
from a wharf deserted by fisheries
but still cracked for a living
by a few poor and hardy Portuguese
whose risky ships
sometimes washed up piecemeal.
Before he left, we talked
about lunch at Jake Wirth's,
doctor's orders, P'town's gentle,
fluttery surf and a vaudeville
anthem hammed up by Durante—
Did you ever have the feeling
that you wanted to go?
Still have the feeling
that you wanted to stay?
His fake leg clamped in place,
Munro timed the sea's big trough
through a week of storms
I dreamed he survived.
A friend in a dream
is not a friend, but a dream,
yet how straight Munro stood
on the street where I touched
the corner of his shoulder
with a feverish relief, saying,
"Everyone here still thinks you're dead."
And how bright the edge
of his pocket knife
when he changed the subject

to a simple engine repair,
twisting his hand at the wrist
as if the angled steel
unlocked a gummy switch,
and the phantom,
seized-up mechanism
began to stir.

Harry's Train

The track's a hilly figure eight,
perfect for the train
to gather speed,
skirt derailment, and enjoy

its fate: no power
but the energy and stasis
of locked circles,
a small winding

across a square foot of rug.
Like a clock's hands,
this train moves only in the present,
and the infinite track

waits for one of us to tire.

Without Warning

A yellow leaf
rushing the asphalt
makes you swerve off the road,
tires grinding the grassy sleeve.
And instead of stopping
you plow along,
finding that getting off like this,
through the grit and straw,
has a sweetness
that you denied
until you kindly turned the wheel
for the sake of a leaf
you thought was alive.
It was as if you died
and then were saved
by a haggard paw
flagging your wet black wheels,
but when you pull back
into the roar
you're a snail
sucking the floor of a ship,
a pear flung through the mist
by a storm,
you're a boy
staring through the sewer grate
at a lost ball,
then stammering home
down a lane
that went so right
and so straight for so long.

The Tears of Mary Magdalene

The tears of Mary Magdalene
washed the feet
of a near god,
and when they touched the earth,
they vanished
just like any other tears.

The mouth of Mary M.
opened like any mouth
when it was astonished or hungry.

She could read Jesus' thoughts
better than he could,
and saved them both from a kiss
that would have made her flushed
with family.

Then she walked the streets again,
no god to urge her on,
no friend, no devil to pay her
for that kiss
that would have toppled Christianity
had it not been placed
on Jesus' feet.

History

If we stare too far ahead
we trip over the feeblest root.

If we look back
we become shadows,
people who pick up accents
from a long stay in a strong country.

If we take too much care,
fearful of the god
whose footfalls we hear approaching,
we go nowhere,

caught in the song
of our age,
the flickering storm of ash
from the raked leaves,

and in the flurry,
a black butterfly
bats the air
as it dips through the cinders.

Which one's on fire?
Which has a home in this world?

The Burned Boy

The burned boy rode the tilt-a-whirl
at our small town fair,
and as his half-shell
shot through the noon sky
I watched his eyes
divide from his head
when he turned the sharp circle
that sped everyone to the false death
promised by the ride.
From the railing where I stood,
all grins raged
into a pulled-back, wind-torn parade,
as if each face
snagged on a thorn and kept going
through the churchyard lot
which drowsed with the chords
of a staticky organ,
booths of fundamentalists and biscuits,
and nothing to do
with our children
in the afternoon
but watch them strain
in their locked seats
against vaulting into the airy gauze
known here as the heavens
and believed to answer every prayer.

Little God

Take a look, little god,
at the pecked and smattered
sill above the street
where thin drunkards
wrap their chests
in a vest of old headlines.
The slate ledge tilts
toward the fire escape's
homemade cross
marking the death
of our super
who jumped to end
his unspeakable ache.
Over here, little god,
I point my index finger
toward the screen
and am not met
by the cushioning touch
of a supreme hand
the way the chapel ceiling
shows it.
Pick me up, little god,
not by the scruff
but in the cupping palm.
Trust that I won't be shunned
by my own kind
after spending a moment
in the air.
Hold me high,
cloaked in a napkin.
Press a bead of water to my lips.

Life Itself

Her smile before she laughed
was all that I could bear,
and when that sound lifted
through the air like a paper plane,
I ached with delight
not only for her gliding shape
but for the things she passed
on her left and right.
She held my hand
in her open hand,
then cupped it like a moth
escorted out
who bangs back at the screen,
heard but unseen.

G 42

I was born two blocks from this bar
where I'm playing one song
over and over and facing
the same streets where I pitched
stickball, fastball, single-double-triple—
games meant to tame boys
on corners waving car antennas
at the sky like stalks of an anemone.
I keep playing the same song,
alone with the words,
the way my fellow barroom weeper
toasts the wall.
The song keeps playing,
and I wait for the same taut note
where I crack in two: you and me,
never linked as a couple
but floaters in that fundamental air
of being just introduced.
I tell you I'm home to visit the folks
and invite you along to see my house,
the school that chilled me as a child,
and the godless flecks
of my grandmother's ashes
sealed in an urn.
You decline because you can't
get away from this
smoke-filled firmament
where you live in a song,
the one that keeps playing
because I play it.

Cleaning Out a Desk

They that wait upon the Lord shall renew their strength

Pay stubs, jeweler's loupe,
a tape of Peggy Lee,
small bean of ivory beasts,
and a mogul's
favorite saying from Isaiah
headlined on the flyer
of the Luce foundation
which I toss
into a carton of keepsakes,
salvaging God's word
with the rules
for begging Mr. Luce
to shake his tablecloth
our way.
It's evening, the office empty,
and I stumble
on a stack of invitations
to a benefit,
each card a magic carpet
to the bouquet-lit banquet
of famous lips kissing hands.
On its other side,
Angel, Patron, Friend,
above a row of boxes
which never saw a benefactor's pen,
each square a small pale field,
a fence around it,
waiting to be scaled.

If He Hadn't

If he hadn't sung, "We're in the money"
in pig latin at the party,

if he hadn't bought a sports car
the color of a dragonfly,

if he hadn't married
a girl from Far Rockaway,

if he hadn't felt it was his duty,

if he hadn't worn
a shimmery suit to the interview,

if he hadn't ridden
the mechanical bull,

if he hadn't ordered one for the road,
changed a flat
and put on another flat,

if he hadn't felt
guided by a saint,

he still would have become
the man

who sold puzzles
forged from horseshoes

at the fair,
a Mr. Chester

who guesses weights,
tells the future for a fee,

and swallows dice
to change the luck of farmers

across the fields
of Johnson County and Buncombe County.

from *The Situation*

Lottery

Pick a number,
any number,
and it will bear
the teeth marks of time.
The day confetti
stippled your shoulders
to keep love
bright and alive;
the year your newborn
son survived.
The two of us riding
the 33 bus
to the birthday bash
where a prophetic
blues band played
"You've Changed."
The magnificent sum
of always, now and still
dealt by the god
who pinched fate
into every living vein.

The Wish Mind

Eternity might very well
be the longed for kiss
you wish would stop,
or the brazen ambition
to live with god,
now folded in the churchyard
with the horse chestnuts.

Eternity could simply
be the thirty shots of radiation
that took you thirty times
until the ending didn't finish,
nor the beginning start.

A girl pats her forehead
with a powder puff,
as if dotting the letter i.
She becomes an x, you change
to o, and the infinite game
ends always in a tie.

Eternity might take the shape
of a werewolf in the wish mind.
The librarian bends over
to look up a skirt.
The howl is strong
and we hear it forever.

Or maybe it's the dominating
seesaw in the center
of the playground,
whose rusty fulcrum squeals
to the children:
Life is long, William.
Life is short, Kate.

No Name for It

A full shot glass in the desert,
shimmering on the bar of the Mirage.

An aged singer back on her feet,
dressed in gold like an autumn leaf.

Someone covers your eyes from behind,
a kindred sport waiting for his change.

It's before soon and after late,
John Gerard,

when you spurn the stiff lie
of sobriety, and your soul lifts

from its trustworthy script.
The blind greeting, jocular and kind,

asks a question you can't answer
Mr. S.,

and because you cannot guess
who's there,

you do not guess.

After a Death

The merciful cushion
of early dark,
the banshee dusk
and waterfall roar
of a steel shaker
draining ice,
the night, the gin,
the FM station's
sanctimonious violin
call to life
the one who died.
His mourners share
a pain so great
they speak the same
and sit together
knee to knee,
the hand of hurt youth
on the arm of the old country.
We walk his wife
across the lawn
where an orange moth,
a sister underwing,
shifts in the black-gowned breeze
as it curtsies to each soul
on the top rung of grief.

Academic

I see straight through myself
and into the no mirror.

A frame stares back,
announcing the time: late.
And the temperature:
still warm.

I recognize the calm
bystander's snowy face,
the handwriting on the blackboard

where chalk dust
from the names of the present
falls to the ledge
toward those who have disappeared.

Song of the Lost and Found

Where does the weight
of the cut branch go
when it returns as driftwood
to the squalling beach?

Do lilies know they last
just a day?

Is the mockingbird praying
for a voice of his own,
or does he rejoice
that worms are blind?

If you find your pen
in the lost and found,
your dog in the pound,
a strong friend
under a mound of clay
too soon,
what do you say?

Time's a wick, a fuse,
a trick to see
if you can shake off
loss and claim,
and dance in pain?

Fishing

I put down the phone and decide
to go fishing,
tired of the noise in my hand.

The rod is ready. Line spins
toward the charging sky
and into the pockmarked sea.

The silver lure thinks everyone has a price.

The fish say the price today is too high.

The sun remains neutral.
Its fight is with the earth
over who will last longer.

I cast and cast into the celestial drink
while the voice of the beyond
speaks through the tide.

I remain on shore
but divide from the man
wiping the sun from his skin
with a heartsick flag.

One side of the brain
hears sadness
in the tingling buoys.
The other says: don't project.

I stand back
and perform that cruel gymnastic
for the soul:
I take a good look at myself.

And I begin to laugh
until I am whole again,
until I know it's not funny.

Three Shards

At certain times of day
the lure displays itself
too loudly. Too proud
the triple treble hooks,
too bright the lacquered
shank of snare
flashing through a school
of bass, an invitation
pressed and passed.
At times like this,
it's best to join those
collecting stones
and shells and sticks,
reminders that
we won't survive
even as we resist
the pull to go beyond
where we belong,
like fish.
Flat stones taken home,
no voice or song,
but strong, heavy playing cards
facedown on a shelf
for us to touch in comfort,
not alarm—for that,
we have the phone
whose ring at certain times
means just one thing.

Thou Sayest

With winter came surprising deaths
and the predictable obituaries
of those closer to stone
than to breath.

The deepest snow does not ask the plow,
thou sayest.

Rope saved to hang himself,
a pack of leggy cards—
these secrets broke
from my neighbor's chest of drawers
when he dropped
between a shovel and a pail of salt.

We watch them die until we die, thou sayest.

Parallel rows in the snow
from the unlifted feet of the old,
craters in the script of their signatures. . . .

We only live so long with those we love,
thou sayest.

"I've got a lovely bunch of coconuts,"
my mother chirps at the bars of a keet cage,
"Roll-a, bowl-a, ball-a-penny-a-pitch,"
my father replies from his spot in the shade.

A bleached nurse praises
their joyful way
of counting back from a hundred.

They're yours until you think they're mine,
thou sayest.

Lilacs

We call their scent unworldly
though all scent is earth-bred:

the perfumed parade down Fifth,
the dog's shoulder

flounced against the carcass
of a fox.

Fuming branches
near the flagstones

transform the wind
the way a shy mouth

puckers in the snap
of pleasure.

Lilacs owe their lives
to the rain and sun,

and when there's thunder
at the door,

they enter
without knocking.

The Boy Whose Parents Drink

The boy whose parents drink
brings a favorite toy
to the lull
between the aimed cup
and the tea-stained wall.
He stands on the carpet
holding a ball that blinks,
a light he thinks will calm the room.

The boy whose parents drink
leaves broken glass
in the school mail slot
then bangs his forehead
on the floor,
hard and harder
for bigger laughs.

The boy whose parents drink
is called to pick the one
he'll live with:
the father who pounds out
lightbulbs with his fist,
or the mother whose shelf
of knickknacks tumbles
when she clips her crystal
with a countering swipe.

The boy whose parents drink
misses drinking
with his drinking father,
just a sip.
As his father opens the car door,
the boy whose parents drink
says, *Bye, Dad* over and over
until nightfall,

when he lies in bed
and makes deals
with the ceiling.

The boy whose parents drink
gets his wish
and does so well in math
a leaning teacher
beams over him
while the class lines up.
Pointing to the zero,
the boy whose parents drink
climbs through it and disappears.

Giovanni Bertolotti

1876–1928

My mother's hand, a cursive trained by nuns,
wrote, "Found downstairs—you can discard"
across the packet of her father's death:

obit, vital certificate, little filler
from the *Mirror*'s back pages—
flint phrases yanked from a trough

of stiff-brimmed prose and the doleful tones
of a medical examiner. No word of wife
or child, just that he fell six flights

from his perch on a scaffold.
Rain brings out a roofer's best and worst
and my mother once drew for us the pitch

of the sugar refinery's tall boiler house,
where a shining statue of Jack Frost
pranced the sky in a pointy hat,

tossing handfuls of pure granules
from a pouch. Should I describe
my grandmother's life, left with eight kids?

Instead I'll end with the snow-white sprite
who did not become "a victim of the weather,"
as the tabloid's squib portrayed

this immigrant leaving his beginnings
near Rome only to land in a railroad car
of pig iron in Edgewater, N. J.,

a town consigned to have its losses
sweetened by an elf, from bay
to bridge, from street to sister street.

Symptomatic

Pleased simply to recall
the chestnuts
gathered in a pall of rain.

Happy just to breathe a bit
the fragrance
that we once consumed.

Can you live with this,
the voices running toward you
from a glass of wine,
the rinsings of the past?

Do you secretly envy
the rush of fisticuffs
near the bar door,
the world of flying forearms,

the men and women
who thunder their way,
while the rest mull the paths
their lives became?

Wouldn't you want to see once more
the rows of corn on Wunderstrand Farm,
the clouds above a boxcar
that jumped the track?

Ladies and gentlemen of the jury,
what is the word for regret?

In the Radiation Oncology Waiting Room

Massachusetts General Hospital

With my small problem, I'm like the vandal
jailed for carving nicknames on a bench
while the rest are facing heavier time.
We stare at the aquarium's
cruel centerpiece of brain coral,
and the brass plaque memorializing,
of all names, Tom Dooley.
Why is the girl in the red sweatshirt crying?
Her mother's hand softly touches her hood,
and softly her small brother scans the room,
unmoved, until the explanations come.
Volunteers offer juice or music,
and the man beside me wears a shirt
that would go unnoticed anywhere but here,
So many books, so little time. . . .
A patient grabs a rushing doctor by the wrist,
forcing his pain into phrases
honed to snare the man of science.
My neighbor taps his book
and says, "I can't put it down,"
because he needs to know the ending,
unlike the other endings here,
still mysterious, still unsolved.
For the very ill, there's hope
in simple words that signify
the simplest future,
so when the man in a gown
extends directions to his seaside home,
we picture it before us,
the highway and the bridge,
the exit curving to land's end,
the turn at the overflowing forsythia
that no one's missed yet.

Prayer Without a God

I'm not your sparrow,
Father X,
though I've been scuffing
patio dust
while you majestically
direct the bees
through swollen lilac sprigs.
Bad god, jaunty god,
all-knowing but forgetful god
of the fractious millimeters
that grow on the brain
without purpose
but change everything,
this is to remind you
I'm still here,
drinking gin in a lawn chair
at gorgeous dusk,
just a twitch of sorrow
because you promised
to notice every sparrow,
and then ignored
the accelerating tumor
and the glass sky
that blinds
the ounce of feathers
to its own reflection.

The Healer

The healer said look inward
at the pain, and see
how firm or bright or loud.
I found a garden in full term,
a path of fronds and flowers
leading to the tumor chewed
by rays but still unfazed
and changed into a lily
fanged with petals
so grotesquely whorled
it's called the Scatterbrain.
Is this what the healer
had in mind,
to find a vaudevillian
in a killer's trance?
I kept up the drill,
my fate fused with this face
that breathed a scent
so strong from summer warmth
I heard bees humming
"Hey Jude,"
and watched a jacket
flying on a nearby line,
one sleeve blown
across the collar
as if shielding its sight
from danger above or below.
In tumor town, you never
know what's next.

The Situation

It's tough, isn't it, star,
to be harangued
by every strain
of brimming heart?

It's hard, isn't it, moon,
when crowds fidget
with their swizzle sticks
as you brighten the bay?

And head, doesn't it hurt
when love ignites
its pesky orbit
and all logic strays?

Hot, isn't it, sun?

Admit it's a relief, shade,
to wear camouflage
while the flamboyant
fade away.

Go ahead, god,
and blame this mess
of blood
and flesh on free will.

That's life, isn't it, death,
when guardrails
along the steep drive home
bristle with wreaths and bouquets?

I Dreamt I Went to Hell with Charles Schwab

He promised me a sail on his Swan
but off the bay
he steered wrong
and soon we faced a fork
swung by the Dark One.
Charles had the tender jowls
of a new senator,
no rent worries ever pitched
their tents there,
packed up, pitched again.
The greasy, dented cheeks of Satan
mirrored my own lumped
and pointy features, no symmetry.
He asked us to explain who had touched
our lives, moved us most, fathered
our fates, the friends who failed us.
Charles confessed first: he never
had a second thought, just pounced.
As for me, I had only second thoughts,
and therefore never. . . .
For these crimes
we were condemned
to fathom each other through a kiss.
Charles understood me right away:
burnt coffee, aspirin, envy.
The rich man tasted familiar, like sucking
a penny, a miniature copper mine,
blood from a fishhook wound,
and the fish, and the hook, and the wound.

Uncle Dugan

A van knocked down the kid playing tag.
The rest of us stood on a manhole cover
above Brooklyn's slurring waste
and beneath the elevated train

that sawed the sun and moon in two.
The driver waved a fifth
of Four Roses like a bad wand
and we disappeared

while tenements emptied to the curb
where Alice Gallon sang "Chantilly Lace"
until her mother slapped
her face with a sauce spoon

with some tomato sauce still on it.
I went home to parts of a steer
bobbing in broth, and Uncle Dugan
exhaling Pall Malls toward

the teardrop chandelier and drinking
Heaven Hill from the bottle.
He said one law demands we eat well
but another keeps food from the poor,

that I was lucky I stayed put
on the iron disk
above Smith Street's suds and shit,
but should know

that even though I'm safe
before a placemat and a spoon,
no drink or art is strong enough
to undermine the fact

that every victim
once inhabited the crowd
of witnesses like you
and you and you.

Uncle Grossman

Uncle Grossman quotes the Greeks and the gods
and says the Great One knows when a feather
falls to a field, then he clears his throat
with the sound of a brake yanked into place.
Grossman, our childless nuncle, bumps
his avuncular head hard against the bird feeder.
As seed fills his fedora's rim, he says,
*Pain makes a world that would not exist
except for pain.* On the way to dinner,
Uncle Grossman describes his current loves,
a woman with five bulldogs, and the nurse
who sneaks him endless Xanax.
Life is comic, he says, and *life is tragic.*
Uncle G. orders his favorite dish, Veal P.,
but does not recommend it.
Although our uncle has not been born again,
he booms with the strength of the just born
against white chocolate, the rosary,
and Galileo's fate. When a small nephew
asks us to drive faster, his uncle states,
*No matter how many cars you pass,
you cannot pass the car ahead of you.*
It's a rainy evening when we see him to the bus.
The long aisle of windows steams,
and we wave goodbye to Uncle Grossman
through the little circle of clarity
he keeps rubbing clean with the heel of his fist.

I Think Continually of Those Not Asked to Dance

I think continually
of those not asked to dance:
the blossoms yearning
in magnolia trees,
the sleek stockings
of the waitress
standing on a stool
to change a dying bulb,
the pink-white petal in her hair
eloped from the row
on Commonwealth
to the parade
of flesh and blood below.
The daring flower dares
all hands to tilt
toward her pulled-back part,
but as she stretches higher
I board a train
that climbs straight up
her nylon seam.
No conductor takes tickets
or calls out the stop
for the Tea for Two Cafe,
so I am far away
when she steps down
and the wayward petal
seesaws to the floor.
We watch it fall,
those who found life
in that silken wing,
while she looks at us
with the same grave face
she gave the flickering light
before it died.

Ghazal: My Way

An empty dinghy called *The Crouton* drifts our way.
The boy swimming after it hears us pointing out its way.

I stagger from the blanket we set neatly in the sand
and wade into the ocean that takes our breath away.

I rethink my marriage, the time of day, our children
clawing at the blisters on their legs, the jam we put away

in early morning which now gushes from the bread,
and for a second I feel an ache for shore, but I'm carried away

by a crazy wanderlust for the tides of yesterday, when a sleek girl
poured tequila, scattered salt around our wrists and said, *let's get away*

from here, but I didn't go, I stayed as if an anchor or a pier
held me in place, unlike finding myself out deep, going every which way

after the dinghy, when I used to have big dreams: ocean liners,
ports of call, an at-your-service captain in the gangway.

Then I'm distracted by a glamorous kite that seems to enjoy
being shaken through the sky, going the wind's way

with abandon, fighting the pull that binds it to the hand.
And I feel rivaled by the lost boat, the feisty kite, and regret my way

has always been to stay on shore, until now when I jumped
to help track down the dinghy that drifted away,

leaving me in freezing water, holding a rope, saying, *John,*
John, you're talking to yourself again, the coward's way.

Aisle 8

I lift a banged can
in the aisle of banged cans,

and a shape stares back,
a face I recognize,

someone I've seen
maneuvering

crumpled aluminum
tons at the dump,

a punch-drunk
heavyweight

led by his father
who escorts the ruined giant

everywhere,
to get the paper,

a bag of grass,
his son still trying to duck

a hemorrhaging past
as he suddenly drops low

at the newsstand.
His head wanders

above his body
like the splayed skull

of a dinner plate dahlia
in the fall wind.

And though it may be ugly,
a fumbled label

in a label-proud world,
it holds a torn corner

of truth, and begins to sing:
If you love me, say so.

If you don't love me, say so.
If you love me and are afraid

to say so, squeeze out my story,
but don't keep me waiting

in this cold convulsive light too long,
because here comes the nightman.

Warmest Personal Regards

Above her name
on the note,
she wrote,
Warmest Personal Regards.
Seven syllables,
ignoring my want
of her,
and my will.
Warm, Warmer,
Warmest—
no matter how I stretch it,
it turns out
like the white walls
of my bedroom
where vitreous floaters
go insane,
and her perfume
makes a museum
of the pillowcase.
All this
come about
from her name
on the note.

Tinnitus

Not the ocean's stutter in a storm,
but the tunneling
of sullen low-tide crabs
lisping Velasquez, Vichyssoise,
Chardonnay and Charlemagne—
a chorus kept in time
by the metronomic ping
of a pong ball
against plate glass
about to loosen
in its frame.
And when you think
it can't get worse,
there's the thip and click
of TV trays unfolding
onto the dewy
wall-to-wall in 1958
as Perry Como sings
his theme designed to lift
each soul from its swamp,
"Dream Along with Me,
I'm on my Way to a Star."

Nothing More

In the back of the cab
I found a badge,
a fake star
to scare the pants off
people already scared.
And flashing that spark
in the woolen dusk,
I said what I could
never say by day,
that I miss your spry
untimely touch,
the way our breathing
tangled and unfurled.
I said, I would . . .
but you kissed me with a kiss
even a heartsick
lack love would ignore,
a consolation kiss, the kiss you whisk
your sister on Christmas,
a kiss that promised nothing,
approached on a small drift
and sailed through the uprights,
tying the score.
Then the avenue seemed darkest,
the stoplights scarlet,
and our driver,
neither priest nor witness,
as you opened the door.

Addendum

I don't have any secrets
unless she was my secret
that summer of rain
the hydrangeas gained weight,
and tourists walked the shore

in shorts eaten by moths,
the shaggy pets of summer's hearth.
To her, summer was a simple
addendum to the overworked year.
A porch. A reaching out,

an act of pity granted
by the god of summer.
But pity, like a summer kiss,
like a kiss on the porch
in summer,

and the porch itself,
extends just so far.
Twin insomniacs hijacked
my sleep that summer:
one who snapped

at the purring brain;
the other who planned
a change at summer's end
and blinked like phosphor
through the clenching dark.

I don't have any secrets
unless she was my secret
that month I rode a drop of rain
down her freckled back
as it fled the summer.

Standing under an awning,
why did everyone running by
seem lost,
and summer so long?
And summer so very long?